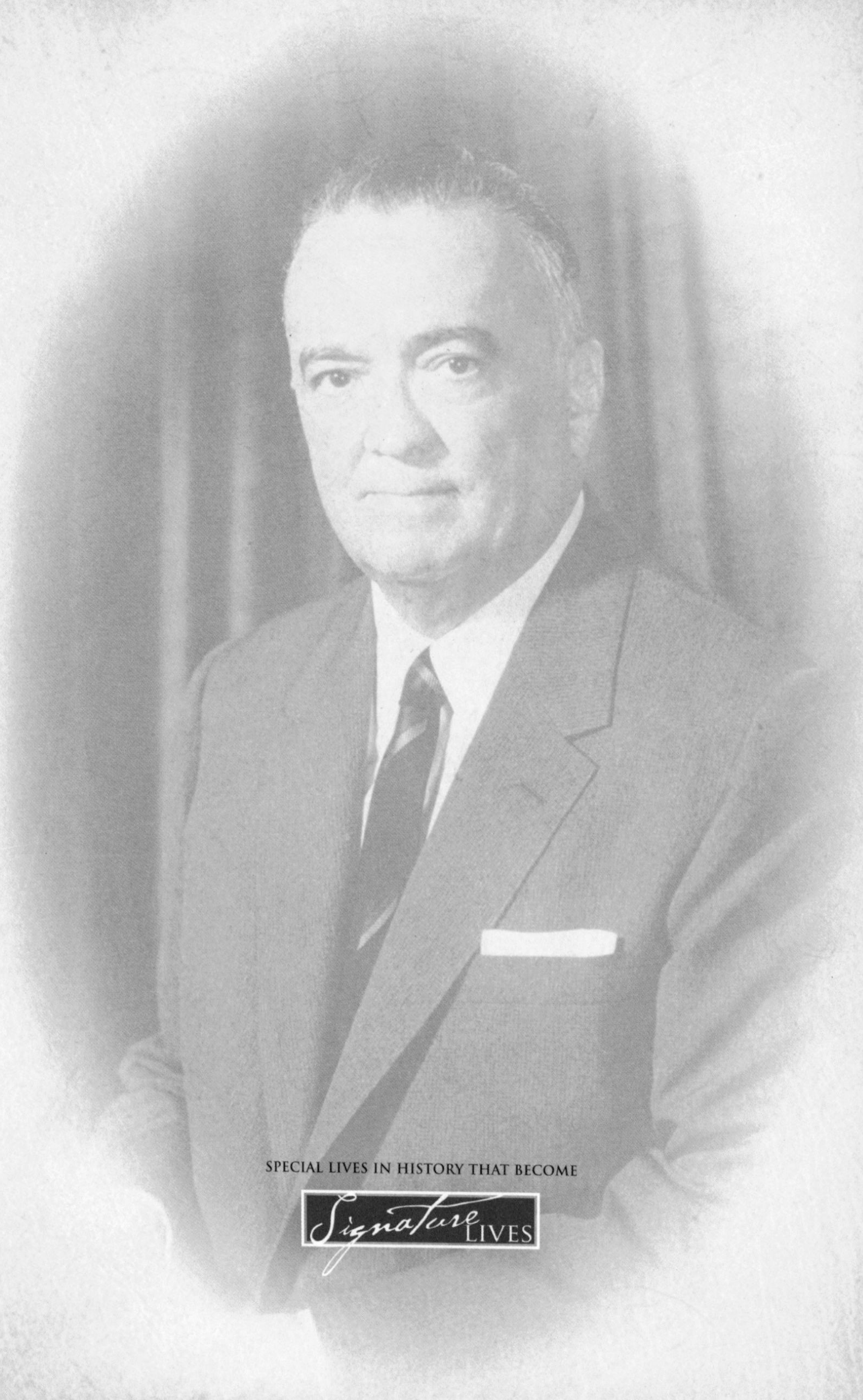

SPECIAL LIVES IN HISTORY THAT BECOME

Signature LIVES

J. EDGAR
HOOVER

CONTROVERSIAL FBI DIRECTOR

by Kevin Cunningham

Content Adviser: Walter E. Burdick, Ph.D.,
Professor and Department Chair,
Department of History,
Elmhurst College

Reading Adviser: Rosemary G. Palmer, Ph.D.,
Department of Literacy, College of Education
Boise State University

COMPASS POINT BOOKS  MINNEAPOLIS, MINNESOTA

Compass Point Books
3109 West 50th Street, #115
Minneapolis, MN 55410

Visit Compass Point Books on the Internet at *www.compasspointbooks.com*
or e-mail your request to *custserv@compasspointbooks.com.*

Editor: Jennifer VanVoorst
Lead Designer: Jaime Martens
Photo Researcher: Svetlana Zhurkin
Page Production: Heather Griffin, Bobbie Nuytten
Cartographer: XNR Productions, Inc.
Educational Consultant: Diane Smolinski

Managing Editor: Catherine Neitge
Creative Director: Keith Griffin
Editorial Director: Carol Jones

Library of Congress Cataloging-in-Publication Data
Cunningham, Kevin, 1966–
    J. Edgar Hoover: controversial FBI director / By Kevin Cunningham.
        p. cm. — (Signature lives)
    Includes bibliographical references and index.
    ISBN 0-7565-0997-1 (hardcover)
    1. Hoover, J. Edgar (John Edgar), 1895–1972—Juvenile literature. 2.
United States. Federal Bureau of Investigation—Biography—Juvenile liter-
ature. 3. Police—United States—Biography—Juvenile literature. 4.
Government executives—United States—Biography—Juvenile literature.
I. Title. II. Series.
HV7911.H6C8 2005
    363.25'092—dc22   2005004614

Signature Lives

MODERN AMERICA

Starting in the late 19th century, advancements in all areas of human activity transformed an old world into a new and modern place. Inventions prompted rapid shifts in lifestyle, and scientific discoveries began to alter the way humanity viewed itself. Beginning with World War I, warfare took place on a global scale, and ideas such as nationalism and communism showed that countries were taking a larger view of their place in the world. The combination of all these changes continues to produce what we know as the modern world.

Table of Contents

WANTED

JOHN HERBERT DILLINGER

On June 23, 1934, HOMER S. CUMMINGS, Attorney General of the United States, under the authority vested in him by an Act of Congress approved June 6, 1934, offered a reward of

$10,000.00

for the capture of John Herbert Dillinger or a reward of

$5,000.00

for information leading to the arrest of John Herbert Dillinger.

DESCRIPTION

Age, 32 years; Height, 5 feet 7-1/8 inches; Weight, 153 pounds; Build, medium; Hair, medium chestnut; Eyes, grey; Complexion, medium; Occupation, machinist; Marks and scars, 1/2 inch scar back left hand, scar middle upper lip, brown mole between eyebrows.

All claims to any of the aforesaid rewards and all questions and disputes that may arise as among claimants to the foregoing rewards shall be passed upon by the Attorney General and his decisions shall be final and conclusive. The right is reserved to divide and allocate portions of any of said rewards as between several claimants. No part of the aforesaid rewards shall be paid to any official or employee of the Department of Justice.

If you are in possession of any information concerning the whereabouts of John Herbert Dillinger, communicate immediately by telephone or telegraph collect to the nearest office of the Division of Investigation, United States Department of Justice, the local addresses of which are set forth on the reverse side of this notice.

JOHN EDGAR HOOVER, DIRECTOR,
DIVISION OF INVESTIGATION,
UNITED STATES DEPARTMENT OF JUSTICE,
WASHINGTON, D. C.

June 25, 1934

1 PUBLIC ENEMY NUMBER ONE

❧⤜✦⤛❧

In March 1934, newspapers in Indiana ran a photo of robber John Dillinger arm in arm with the local prosecutor. "I am not a bad fellow, ladies and gentlemen," Dillinger announced. "I was just an unfortunate boy who started wrong." Journalists ate it up. News stories mentioned the bank robber's good diction and friendly personality.

As director of the U.S. government's top law enforcement office, J. Edgar Hoover said no photo ever made him angrier. Still, John Dillinger offered Hoover the big case his Department of Investigation needed. In fact, Dillinger became the most famous case of Hoover's career.

Known as "Handsome Johnny," Dillinger's good looks and flair caught the public's imagination. That

America's "Public Enemy Number One" in 1934, John Dillinger was wanted on charges of robbery and murder.

he robbed banks helped his reputation. During the Great Depression, banks were more unpopular than crooks. Bank closings had wiped out the savings of millions of people. Those banks still open took back farms, houses, and other property when those who had lost their jobs could not make payments. Dillinger threatened to become a folk hero. As one letter to a newspaper put it, "He wasn't worse than banks and politicians who took the poor people's money. Dillinger did not rob poor people. He robbed those who became rich by robbing the poor."

Dillinger became Hoover's problem on March 3, 1934. That day, he bluffed his way out of an Indiana jail with a fake wooden gun, stole the sheriff's Ford, and headed for Chicago. Because it was a federal crime to drive a stolen vehicle across state lines, the Department of Investigation (DOI) now had an official reason to join the case.

On April 22, Melvin Purvis, the agent in charge of the Chicago office, learned the Dillinger gang's whereabouts: the Little Bohemia Resort in northern Wisconsin. Purvis gathered every agent he could and flew north. Hoover, sure of success, called reporters and told them to hold space for news of Dillinger's capture.

The capture turned into a disaster. Purvis' men shot three innocent bystanders, killing one, while the Dillinger gang escaped out the back. Nearby, two agents and a local lawman stumbled onto the gang's most vicious member, "Baby Face" Nelson. Nelson killed one man and wounded the other two before getting away.

Little Bohemia became a scandal. Critics called for Hoover's demotion or resignation. Meanwhile, Dillinger seemed to be every-where. Sightings came in from around the world. Stories spread about his exploits. He supposedly wrote a letter to automaker Henry Ford, thanking him for building such fast getaway cars. The public followed Dillinger's pursuit as if watching a real-life gangster movie. Hoover added to the drama by naming Dillinger "Public Enemy Number One" and offering a $10,000 reward for his capture.

As director of the DOI, it was J. Edgar Hoover's job to bring gangsters to justice.

Purvis redeemed himself July 22. Acting on a tip from one of Dillinger's friends, he and a team of agents waited outside the Biograph, a movie theater on Chicago's North Side. When Dillinger and his companions came outside, Purvis shouted for

Dillinger to surrender. Charles Winstead, one of the agents on the scene, remembered:

Chicago residents flocked to the Biograph theater after the shooting.

> *I knew right away it was Dillinger. ...*
> *He whirled around and reached for his*
> *right front pocket. He started running*

sideways toward an alley. When a guy like Dillinger reaches for his pocket, you don't ask questions. ... The first shot hit him. He started spinning like a top.

Public Enemy Number One was dead. Although the press tried to make Purvis the hero, Hoover had other ideas. He put out an "official" version that overlooked the case's many errors, the lucky breaks, and Purvis' role. Soon that was the only version people remembered.

Dillinger remained a lifelong fascination for Hoover. A copy of a mask made of the deceased criminal's face always remained on display in the room outside Hoover's office. So did the eyeglasses and cigar taken from Dillinger's body.

The Dillinger case brought fame and new respect to Hoover's Department of Investigation. Still, it was Hoover's organizational leadership more than cases that transformed the DOI from a small federal task force into the Federal Bureau of Investigation (FBI), the most modern crime-fighting unit in the world. Though his long career was plagued with controversy, few would disagree that J. Edgar Hoover played a large role in helping redefine the role of law enforcement in the 20th century. ✍

2 EARLY YEARS

೧೯‿೨೬

John Edgar Hoover was born on New Year's Day, 1895, at 413 Seward Square Southeast in Washington, D.C. Both sides of his family had roots in the city and in government service. Edgar's father, Dickerson Naylor Hoover, grew up in Washington, D.C., during the Civil War, when Confederate troops threatened the city. As an adult he worked in a government print shop, as his own father had done. But the roots went deeper. Family history had it that Edgar's great-grandfather worked on the construction of the Capitol building.

Edgar's mother, Annie Margaret Scheitlin Hoover, also had a family history in government service. Her grandfather was a Swiss immigrant who served as Switzerland's consul to the United States from 1853

People in Washington, D.C., traveled by streetcar around the turn of the 20th century.

to 1864. When he retired, his son—Edgar's grandfather—stepped into the job. With the exception of her high school years, which she spent in Switzerland, Annie lived in Seward Square her entire life.

Edgar was the youngest of four children. His brother Dickerson Junior, nicknamed Dick, was 15 years older; his sister Lillian was 13 years older. Three-year-old Sadie Marguerite had died of diphtheria before Edgar was born. The rest of the family preferred the nickname "J.E.," but Annie called her youngest child Edgar.

Edgar's neighborhood was one of many occupied by government workers and their families. The Hoovers lived in a modest three-bedroom house. Their neighbors were—like the Hoovers— Protestant, middle-class, and white. The only African-Americans were the servants. Seward Square, like the rest of the city, was segregated. Many Washington, D.C., residents considered racism respectable. Jim Crow laws soon made segregation the law, both in Washington and throughout the country. As black writer Charles W. Chestnut wrote in 1903, "The rights of Negroes are at a lower ebb than at any time during the thirty-five years of their freedom, and the race prejudice more intense and uncompromising."

> *Jim Crow laws refer to laws that segregate blacks from whites. In the 1880s, racial segregation was legalized in many parts of the South. The term Jim Crow came from the name of a black character in a popular song from the 1830s.*

The family lavished love and attention on Edgar. His father spent his free time studying or brewing up homemade ginger ale in the basement for Edgar and his friends. His mother was more interested in law and order in the household. She was the disciplinarian, and her drive to punish wrongdoing and reward obedience eventually became part of Edgar's own personality. His mother also had a domineering personality, and she pushed Edgar to learn. By age 2, he knew the alphabet. By age 3, he could print words. He entered elementary school able to read. It helped that he enjoyed reading, because Brent Elementary was known for being tough. Teachers taught the classics. Prayer and Bible study were part of the school day as well.

Though Edgar did well in school, he began stuttering in first grade. His father thought it would work itself out, but his mother sought treatment. The solution proposed was that he talk faster. Edgar practiced in his room for hours with a single-mindedness he would show throughout his life. It took

Hoover grew up in the Washington, D.C., neighborhood of Seward Square.

time to master fluent speaking. Even in adulthood he needed to practice. But he conquered the stutter enough that he became the star of his debate team in high school.

In many ways Edgar was a typical child. He loved sports, particularly baseball and swimming. He printed up jokes, neighborhood gossip, and health advice in a newspaper that he sold for 1 cent. In 1909, he traveled to see the Wright brothers demonstrate a new airplane and shook Orville Wright's hand. Encouraged to learn by his mother, Edgar eagerly read history, geography, and religion. Around age 11, he also began to keep a diary. In it, he detailed his own adventures, the weather conditions, his clothes sizes, the money he made and spent—almost anything that interested him.

Brothers Wilbur and Orville Wright built the first successful airplane. On December 17, 1903, they made the world's first flight near Kitty Hawk, North Carolina. With Orville at the controls, the plane flew 120 feet (37 meters) and was in the air for 12 seconds. The Wrights made three more flights that day.

Religion played a strong role in Edgar's life. "I always had to go to Sunday school," he remembered as an adult. "I was given a little Testament for attendance on fifty-two consecutive Sundays and it was one of my treasures. I still have it." He sang in the choir at the Church of the Reformation, a nearby Lutheran church. On Sundays, his grandmother

> When Edgar was 13 years old, a boil on his nose became infected. When the infection finally healed, it left a scar, creating a permanent indentation in his nose. As an adult, he encouraged the more dramatic story that he injured his nose while participating in a sporting event.

Margaret Scheitlin visited and sometimes brought John Hitz, Edgar's imposing great-uncle. Known for his strong faith, Hitz read from the Bible in his thundering voice.

Although Edgar's family was Lutheran, one of his greatest influences growing up was Dr. Donald Campbell MacLeod, a clergyman who ran the First Presbyterian Church, one of the city's most historic churches. Edgar idolized MacLeod. He admired the clergyman's sense of duty and clear-cut view of right and wrong. When Edgar's brother, Dick, became a leader at First Presbyterian, Edgar followed him to the new church. According to his diary, Edgar took first communion there on September 11, 1910, and he taught Sunday school at First Presbyterian throughout his teen years. At one time, he even considered becoming a minister himself.

Edgar's first steady job was carrying groceries. Each trip earned him a 10 cent tip. He claimed this was the origin of his nickname, "Speed":

> *In those days markets did not hire delivery boys, but I discovered that if one stood*

outside a store, a customer laden with purchases would happily accept a helping hand and gratefully tip anyone who aided with a heavy load. ... I realized that the quicker I could complete each chore, the more money I could earn, so I spent most of my time running.

Others claimed Edgar got the nickname because he talked so fast—his way of not just beating his stutter but controlling a conversation.

Edgar attended Central High School, the city's oldest and most challenging public school. It was also for whites only. There, Edgar took part in many school activities. Too small for football, he ran track. He sang in the choir, and in his sophomore year he joined the debate team. This was quite a challenge for a stutterer, but he practiced debating every day, and in his junior year, Edgar led the team to an undefeated season. Debate taught him how to keep a cool head, gave him an eye for detail, and showed him how to attack the weak points of an argument. Whether in private meetings or before Congress, he would put those skills to use for the rest of his life.

But the school's cadet corps was Edgar's true love. This organization provided leadership training to prepare young men and women for military service to the nation. Everything about the cadets appealed to Edgar's sense of order. High school teams throughout the area drilled in complicated marches and competed in tournaments. Practices were held three times a week, and cadets wore military-style uniforms. By his senior year, Edgar had risen to captain of the squad.

In the midst of all Edgar's activity, tragedy struck the family. For years his father had suffered from depression. Unable to sleep, and prone to nervousness, he finally had a breakdown during Edgar's senior year. Edgar never spoke of it—not even in his diary. When his father returned home from the hospital several months later, his memory was damaged. He continued to suffer from severe depression for the rest of his life.

As Edgar's senior year wound to a close, he led the cadet corps in President Woodrow Wilson's inaugural parade. That year the annual cadet dance took place at the Cairo Hotel, the tallest in Washington. Edgar kept his dance card from the evening his entire life. Yet it was totally blank. His niece Margaret, whom he saw often in those years, thought she knew why: "[Edgar] had a fear of becoming too personally involved with people." Though his classmates chose him to give the graduation speech, Edgar would not continue a single friendship from school into adult life.

Edgar wanted to study law, so college was the next step. He turned down a scholarship from the

Crowds gathered in Washington, D.C., for the 1913 inauguration of President Woodrow Wilson.

University of Virginia to attend George Washington University (GWU) in Washington, D.C. Attending GWU had two advantages. First, he could live at home. Second, it offered law classes at night. That allowed him to hold a day job.

While in college Edgar worked at the Library of Congress, the government library that holds nearly every work published in the United States.

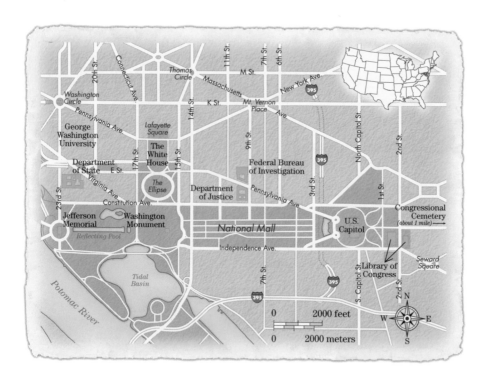

Government service was a comfortable fit for Edgar. His father and grandfather had worked for the government, and his older brother worked for the U.S. Steamboat Inspection Service. He understood the lifestyle of a government worker and had learned from his relatives about the way one rose to power in the federal system.

The Library of Congress was an especially good fit for Edgar as well. As a messenger, he earned a salary of $360 a year. He was soon promoted to cataloger, however, and then to clerk, with a salary of almost twice his original pay. At the library, Edgar learned how librarians organized books, magazines, newspapers, and government documents. He learned the numbering system they used to identify and track each item the library possessed. Through this work, Edgar developed his talent for collecting and organizing information, a skill that would later become a hallmark of his career.

Edgar put work aside long enough to enjoy a social life. While at George Washington University, he joined a fraternity, a social organization for male students. Still, fraternity members remembered that the serious and driven Edgar often looked down on some of their fun.

In 1916, Edgar received his bachelor's degree in law and continued to study for a master's degree. By the time J. Edgar Hoover graduated in 1917 with his master's degree, he was a four-year veteran of government service—a good head start on a career. He passed the exam to become a lawyer on July 25, 1917. The next day he was hired as a clerk at the Department of Justice, known around Washington, D.C., as the DOJ.

Chapter
3 THE RED SCARE

❧❧❧

In 1917, the United States entered World War I against Germany, Austria-Hungary, and their allies. At this point, the war had raged in Europe for nearly three years. While U.S. soldiers packed for Europe, the Department of Justice hunted down enemy spies and sympathizers living in the United States. People of German descent were considered especially dangerous.

Hoover threw himself into 12-hour workdays, including nights and Sundays. Eventually he moved into a job with the DOJ's Alien Enemy Bureau. There he studied cases of Germans, Austro-Hungarians, and other "enemy aliens" living in the United States. Patriotic feelings ran strong in the DOJ. Calling the U.S. president names or questioning the war was

In 1920, federal agents raided the offices of a newspaper said to support radical viewpoints.

grounds for arrest. Such "crimes" sent many Germans and Austro-Hungarians to jail until the end of the war.

The Alien Enemy Bureau did not use the usual court system to try its cases. Instead, government officials—not a judge or a jury—decided the sentence. Hoover would soon help use that kind of efficient and unfair system against another enemy, one that dominated his thoughts and guided his career: communism.

Communism developed in the 19th century as an alternative to the brutal capitalism of the time. In its pure form, all property and goods would be owned communally—that is, by everyone. Communism remained a powerful idea in the early 20th century, in part because it had not been tried yet. That changed in 1917. Communists seized power in Russia. Communists elsewhere declared this was the start of a worldwide revolution. After the war ended in 1918, communist groups across Europe tried to take power in several countries.

Many Americans believed revolution would soon spread to the United States. "Reds"—so called because communists put that color on their flags and often wore it—seemed to be everywhere. So did people with a variety of other radical beliefs. To many, the terms *radical* and *Red* meant not only communists but also anarchists (people who

believed in no government), liberals (people who believed in an active government), and, as one historian humorously remarked, anyone who disagreed with you.

A series of bombings around the country added to the tension. The targets—politicians, judges, and businessmen—had acted or spoken out against radicals or foreigners. Many of the explosives were sent through the mail, and most of them were stopped by the postal service without harm, though one former senator's wife and maid suffered serious injuries when a mail bomb went off in their home. The

In 1917, Vladimir Ilyich Lenin, an early supporter of communism, organized a communist revolution in Russia.

bombing campaign peaked with attacks in eight cities on June 2, 1919. In Washington, D.C., U.S. Attorney General A. Mitchell Palmer had just gone upstairs to bed when a blast shook his house:

> *I heard a crash downstairs as if something had been thrown against the front door. It was followed immediately by an explosion which blew in the front of the house. ... No one inside the house was injured by the explosion. It cracked the upper part of the first story of the house, blew in the front of the lower floor, broke windows, and knocked pictures from the walls.*

Attorney General A. Mitchell Palmer organized a series of raids to capture suspected communists.

Fifty copies of a radical leaflet—and pieces of the bomb—were scattered throughout the neighborhood. The next day, Palmer ordered the DOJ's Bureau of Investigation, a government detective force that investigated federal crimes, to take on communist and radical groups. The period that came to be known as the

"Red Scare" had begun.

As attorney general, Palmer was the top law enforcement official in the country, and he oversaw the work of the Bureau of Investigation. He planned to capture radicals in a series of raids and throw them out of the country before they could appeal the decision. Still, he could not throw out just anyone with radical ideas. United States citizens were free to belong to any group they wished. But foreigners living in the United States lacked that protection.

Palmer hinted that an attempt to overthrow the government was planned for the Fourth of July. The holiday came and went without incident. Palmer continued to issue warnings into the fall. Newspapers played up every new alert—but also criticized Palmer for not doing more to stop the "Red Menace."

Hoover had strong feelings about communism. He said it was the most evil, monstrous conspiracy against man since time began. During his days at the Alien Enemy Bureau, Hoover had begun to keep files on "Reds," radicals, and anyone else opposed to the war. He was recognized as the DOJ's expert on radical groups, and in 1919, Attorney General Palmer asked him to join the Bureau of Investigation. There, Hoover enlarged his wartime files with mailing lists of radical groups and reports from government agencies and police departments.

Suspected "Reds" were placed behind bars, often in crowded and unhealthy conditions.

citizens were released, as were foreigners without any ties to radical groups. Approximately 6,000 went free right away.

The Red Scare began to fall apart. Politicians, the newspapers, and the public soon began to ask questions about the mistakes and poor treatment. By the middle of April 1920, Acting Secretary of Labor Louis F. Post had set hundreds of prisoners free. He accused Palmer of being ignorant of American principles of justice.

Recognizing the need for good media coverage, Hoover put out a stream of bulletins that said the communist uprising in the United States would take place on May 1. When nothing happened, Palmer's supporters said the attorney general had stopped the revolution.

Later in the month, a dozen respected legal figures released a detailed report critical of the raids. The facts were difficult to refute. Hoover responded by opening secret files on the report's authors and ordered BI agents to try to dig up Post's ties to communists. The agents failed to turn up any information that could be used to defend the raids, and Congress and the press turned on Palmer.

Hoover insisted he did not personally support the Palmer raids—that others made the plans and that he only followed orders. Though most historians say otherwise, at the time his denials were accepted as fact. Still, neither Palmer nor Hoover wanted to give up the fight against Reds. In fact, Hoover never gave it up.

The BI, and later the FBI, kept a secret list of thousands of Americans to be rounded up "in case of national emergency." In the 1940s, the government ordered Hoover to get rid of the list. Instead, he changed the name of the list and made it a Bureau secret. One agent said that if all the suspects on the list were rounded up, the Bureau would need a football stadium to hold them all.

Chapter
4 THE 1920S

⤷⟶⟵⤶

The early 1920s were an unhappy time for Hoover. His father died of depression in 1921, and work kept Hoover from spending much time with his mother. Still, Hoover was not alone, even if the only photo on his desk was of his dog. He also had his niece Margaret, his brother Dick's teenage daughter. When Dick's family moved to Maryland, Margaret stayed at Hoover's house while she finished high school in the city. He also spent time with Frank Baughman, a college friend and longtime assistant at the BI. Baughman was a decorated World War I veteran. He was outgoing, while Hoover was shy and something of a loner. Still, the two enjoyed one another's company. They shared meals and movies. Both also liked pricey white linen suits. Hoover, a silk handkerchief

As director of the Department of Justice's Bureau of Investigation, J. Edgar Hoover investigated individuals suspected of violating federal laws.

always in his breast pocket, gained a reputation as a fancy dresser.

Hoover's dedication to work, however, allowed little time for outside interests. He was pushing hard for the assistant director's job at the Bureau of Investigation. Numerous Washington friends recommended him to advisers of the newly elected president, Warren G. Harding. Hoover increased his chances by sharing files that contained information on Harding's political foes. He got the job.

Hoover's direct superior was William J. Burns. As owner of the country's best-known detective agency, Burns had solved several famous cases. He also made a lot of money destroying labor unions for big companies. Burns considered the BI a place to reward political friends with easy government jobs. One of Burns' friends, Gaston B. Means, was a legendary con man. With access to BI files and a badge, Means made a fortune fixing the outcomes of court cases, pardoning criminals (for a price), and selling Hoover's files.

As a result of such activities, the reputation of the Department of Justice began to suffer. Hoover's sense of pride was deeply wounded. He was so ashamed at his department's tarnished reputation that he simply told people he worked for the government, without naming the department.

But corruption was present in the government at

levels much higher than the DOJ. Shortly after taking office, a wave of scandals threatened Harding's
presidency. When the Senate began to investigate,
Burns worked to discredit the Senate investigators.
Although he was angry at what Burns was doing to
the department, Hoover put his personal feelings
aside and helped Burns. Senator Burton K. Wheeler
later hinted at Hoover's methods:

> *Agents of the [DOJ] raided my offices,
> they broke into my offices ... they sta-
> tioned men at my house, surrounded my*

*A Senate com-
mittee was
assembled to
investigate
corruption in
the Harding
administration.*

*house, watched persons who went in and
came out, constantly shadowed me, and
shadowed my wife.*

At least four senators and one representative
received similar treatment.

In August 1923, President Harding died in office
with a year and a half left in his term. When Vice
President Calvin Coolidge became president,
Hoover once again maneuvered to keep his job—
and aimed at a better one. The imposing new attorney general, Harlan Stone, had plans to reform the
BI. Stone had already fired Burns, and when he asked
Hoover to a May 24 meeting, Hoover wondered if he
were about to lose his job.

Instead, Stone asked Hoover to fill in as the tem-
porary acting director of the BI. Over the years
Hoover often repeated his story about the meeting.
He told Stone that he would accept the job with the
following conditions:

*The Bureau must be divorced from poli-
tics and not a catch-all for political hacks.
Appointments must be made on merit.
Second, promotions will be made on
proven ability and the Bureau will be
responsible only to the Attorney General.*

Stone responded, "I wouldn't give it to you under
any other conditions. That's all. Good day."

Attorney General Harlan Fiske Stone was the top official in the Department of Justice.

Stone sent him detailed orders and Hoover threw his great energy into cleaning up the BI. Gaston B. Means, the friend of the former director, was the first to go. Thirty-nine agents left or were fired, and Hoover eliminated half of the office staff.

But Stone wanted more. He imagined the BI as a new kind of professional law enforcement agency. That required Hoover to use his well-known talent for organizing. New rules ordered Bureau offices around the country to use the same filing system—Hoover's. He assessed and graded the performance of all of the agents. Not surprisingly, many did not meet with his approval:

> *Men in charge of some of the field offices had never had any experience in investigative work, but were put there through political influence. I cleaned that crowd out, because they were not competent.*

Hoover developed strict new requirements for dress, training, and behavior. A white shirt, plain tie, and dark suit became the BI agent uniform. Recruits were required to be educated as lawyers or accountants. And drinking alcohol at any time was absolutely forbidden.

Not everything changed, however. Hoover continued to worry about communists. Stone had said:

> *The Bureau of Investigation is not concerned with political or other opinions of individuals. It is concerned only with their conduct and then only such conduct as is forbidden by the laws of the United States.*

Despite Stone's assurances, however, the "political or other opinions" held by people and groups in the United States remained one of Hoover's primary concern.

Hoover met with Roger Baldwin, head of the American Civil Liberties Union (ACLU). Baldwin wanted to know if the BI continued to keep files on so-called radicals and radical organizations, including the ACLU. Not only had the BI stopped, Hoover said, but no ACLU file had ever existed. Hoover's sincerity won over Baldwin. Even Stone was convinced.

In fact, Hoover secretly kept files on the ACLU and did so for the rest of his life. Baldwin also rated a large file. Hoover opened one on Harlan Stone, as well, and continued to add to the file even after Stone became a justice on the Supreme Court.

On December 10, 1924, Stone named Hoover the official director of the BI. Hoover and Baughman, his friend and associate, celebrated by taking their mothers to New York City to see a show. Afterward, they met the famous dancer Fred Astaire—the first of Hoover's many meetings with celebrities. Within 10 years, the director of the BI would be as famous as any of them. 🔊

> *Hoover's boss, Attorney General Harlan Fiske Stone (1872–1946), was appointed to the U.S. Supreme Court in 1925. He served as an associate justice until 1941, when he was appointed chief justice. Though Stone held conservative views, he often ruled to uphold liberal measures. He held the position of chief justice until his death in 1946.*

Chapter
5 GANGSTERS AND G-MEN

ఎలా

In 1929, the U.S. stock market crashed, plunging the United States—and then the world—into an economic depression. Banks and businesses closed, leaving millions of people without their savings— or an income. Many lost their homes and were forced to live in shacks or on the street. By 1932, the Great Depression's unemployment and poverty had exhausted Americans. They elected Franklin D. Roosevelt, who promised them a "New Deal," as president.

In early 1933, while Roosevelt was introducing the first laws that he promised would restore hope to the country, a crime wave hit the Midwest. It included a cast of characters with nicknames like "Pretty Boy" and "Handsome Johnny." On the morning of June 17,

J. Edgar Hoover aims a Thompson submachine gun while taking part in DOI target practice.

1933, four Bureau agents, an Oklahoma police chief, and two local policemen were escorting escaped bank robber Frank Nash back to prison. As the group gathered outside Kansas City's train station, they were ambushed by three men with machine guns. One Bureau agent was killed and two others hurt; the police chief, Kansas City policemen, and Nash all died.

It was the job of the BI to find the killers and bring them to justice. An angry Hoover answered reporters' questions about the massacre via telephone. "We will never stop until we get our men, if it takes ages to accomplish it," Hoover told them. "There will be no letup in this case." Privately he told colleagues, "They must be exterminated, and exterminated by us, and to this end we are dedicating ourselves."

Attorney General Homer S. Cummings recognized the massacre offered an opportunity: Capturing the killers would help restore Americans' faith in government by demonstrating that the Roosevelt administration was working to change the country for the better. And at the moment, catching crooks sounded easier than solving the problems of the Great Depression. Cummings folded the BI into a new Division of Investigation (DOI) and put Hoover in charge. There was one problem, though, and Hoover knew it: The DOI was not up to the job.

Hoover (back center) watched as President Roosevelt signed a tough new crime bill into law.

At the time, the DOI training concentrated on administration—keeping information, dealing with paperwork—rather than conducting criminal investigations. Hoover hired agents based on hard work and a clean-cut appearance, not law enforcement experience. DOI agents could not make arrests or carry firearms. Future DOI assistant director Hugh Clegg, a young agent at the time, remembered:

> *The policeman [would] tell me, "Well, you guard the back and I'll go in the front. You don't have a gun so I'll go in." I've stood at the back door of a house, had [only a brick] in my hand, hoping that [the sus-*

pect] would not come out my way. ... If he'd come out shooting, I had no defense at all.

To get the DOI into shape, Hoover needed experienced lawmen who knew how to track down criminals. With the department's reputation at stake, he went outside the DOI and hired seasoned investigators, many of them ex-policemen. These new agents tended to prefer cowboy clothes to suits and ties. Few had college educations. All carried guns. For once, Hoover had to ignore his long list of rules.

At first, Attorney General Cummings' plan to make the Roosevelt administration look good backfired. The DOI's investigation of the Kansas City massacre quickly became bogged down. Agents overlooked or misplaced key evidence. Agents and local police considered most of the eyewitnesses unreliable. The agents who survived the massacre claimed they had not gotten a look at the murderers.

A second high-profile case also remained unresolved. In late July 1933, a gang led by George

The administration recognized that the DOI was not equipped to wage a war on crime, so over the next year, Congress passed a number of new laws. It redefined certain crimes as federal offenses. For example, it became a federal crime to rob a bank, transport stolen property, assault a government agent, and avoid arrest by crossing state lines. Agents were also now authorized to carry guns, perform searches, and make arrests.

"Machine Gun" Kelly kidnapped rich oilman Charles Urschel. Then Kelly and his wife vanished with their share of the $200,000 ransom. Since kidnapping was a federal crime, Hoover and the DOI pursued the investigation.

Hoover and the DOI faced criticism as both cases dragged on. An article in *Collier's* magazine offered personal criticism as well:

> *The director's appetite for publicity is the talk of the Capitol, although admittedly a peculiar enterprise for a bureau which ... is supposed to operate in secrecy.*
>
> *In appearance, Mr. Hoover looks utterly unlike the storybook sleuth. He is short, fat, businesslike, and walks with a mincing step. His black hair, swarthy skin, and collegiate haircut make him look younger than thirty-eight, but heavy horn-rimmed spectacles give him an air of age and authority. ... A little pompous, he rides in an expensive limousine even if only to a nearby self-serve cafeteria.*

The Kelly case broke first. On September 26, 1933, DOI agents and local police surprised the Kellys in a Memphis farmhouse. George Kelly gave up without a fight, telling agents he had been waiting for them all night. Hoover, aware of the press' hunger for a good story, embellished a bit for

"Machine Gun" Kelly was led away in shackles after his capture by DOI agents.

reporters. In his version, Kelly cried out, "Don't shoot, G-men, don't shoot!" The G-man—or government man—label stuck. Soon everyone was using it.

But the case earned the DOI more than a nickname. The DOI had proved it could catch a big-name criminal. Luck was involved—the mistake-prone Mrs. Kelly had accidentally tipped off authorities—but it did not fit with the story Hoover wished to promote, so no one mentioned it. The case was a law enforcement and public relations success.

The Kansas City situation, however, reached a

controversial end. Early on, authorities had made up a list of suspects. By autumn 1934, one was dead and another in jail. Hoover needed a new prime suspect. Despite a lack of evidence, he named Charles Arthur "Pretty Boy" Floyd and Floyd's partner, Adam Richetti, as the killers.

But Floyd and Richetti had to be found and arrested before they could be tried for the crime. In mid-October, a team of agents led by DOI agent Melvin Purvis shot and killed Floyd in an Ohio field.

"Pretty Boy" Floyd was one of the most famous bank robbers of the time. There was even a song written about him. The evidence against him in the Kansas City case, however, was thin. Much of the DOI's case against Floyd relied on the testimony of a single eyewitness— out of dozens—and the authorities in Kansas City considered her unreliable.

Richetti was caught and put on trial. At the trial, the three survivors of the massacre, previously unsure of what happened, now recalled Floyd and Richetti at the scene. Without a doubt, Floyd and Richetti were criminals, but whether or not either took part in the massacre remains in question to this day. Still, Richetti was eventually executed for the crime.

Almost all of the big-name criminals of the period were now dead or in custody, and Hoover's G-men had earned a new image. The public, the press, and Hollywood saw them as superheroes and J. Edgar Hoover as their brilliant leader—the greatest crime fighter in America. ॐ

FIFTEEN CENTS (IN CANADA, 20c) (Station Later)

August 5, 1935

TIME

The Weekly Newsmagazine

JOHN EDGAR HOOVER

His quarry has a gun in his hand, murder in his heart.
(See NATIONAL AFFAIRS)

Volume XXVI

Number 6

Chapter
6 NATIONAL HERO

⤶⥨✕⥩⤷

Hoover's G-men became a national craze. Millions of American boys carried G-man toy badges and played with G-man toy guns. They joined Junior G-man clubs featured on breakfast cereal boxes and slept each night in G-man pajamas. Hollywood made G-men into movie heroes in films with titles like *Let 'Em Have It*, *Public Enemy's Wife*, and *G-Men*. Hoover used the craze to turn himself into the symbol of the newly named Federal Bureau of Investigation (FBI). In the process, he became a celebrity and a national hero.

Though celebrated for its captures of big-name gangsters like Kelly, Floyd, and Dillinger, the FBI's real effect on law enforcement was quieter and longer lasting. Under Hoover's direction, the Bureau

In 1935, J. Edgar Hoover was featured on the cover of Time *magazine.*

became a central source of information for police departments around the country. Its fingerprint files were by far the largest in the world. Its laboratories analyzed handwriting, ballistics (guns and bullets), and other chemical and forensic evidence. All of these tools were available to any police or sheriff's department in the country, free of charge. Since only the biggest cities had their own labs, the FBI's professional setup made cutting-edge techniques available nationwide.

As always, Hoover had high standards for his agents. They were judged on a long list of traits that included knowledge, accuracy, and attitude. The Bureau also gave them grades in categories that Hoover felt were important, such as personal appearance and the ability to deal with paperwork. Regulations were strict. If an agent got to work one minute late, a note went into his file.

The system could be unfair. Hoover had total control. He was allowed to promote or fire for any reason, including a personal grudge. Unlike many government workers, FBI agents lacked protection if they had trouble with their boss. And since Hoover had a terrible temper, getting on his bad side was a constant risk.

Hoover wanted to promote an image of the Bureau that was professional, scientific, all-American, and honest. So a former New York reporter, Henry Suydam, was hired to tell the press and public the government's version of any story. Hoover had to approve everything Suydam wrote about the Bureau or himself. One press release declared, "J. Edgar Hoover is the personification of every decent minded citizen who wants to live in a world free of criminals."

Hoover and Suydam saw the many ways to use entertainment to promote the FBI. With Hoover's permission, a crime writer named Courtney Ryley Cooper used Bureau files to write a series of popular stories about G-men. All showed G-men pursuing crooks with bravery and ended with the FBI "getting its man." All made it clear that FBI Director J. Edgar Hoover ordered every move. Hoover also lent his support to a detective magazine called *The Feds*. In return, *The Feds* named him "Public Hero Number One."

Hoover also used comic strips to reach kids:

> The value of this sort of thing to the growing boy cannot be overestimated. He is taught that the policeman can be and is his friend, and he learns to see crime in its true light—as something far from

J. Edgar Hoover was so famous that Superman, the Flash, and other members of the DC Comics' Justice Society of America visited him during one of their comic book adventures. The Flash even remarked that Hoover was a "swell guy."

glamorous, something sordid and evil that must be stamped out.

"War On Crime," a comic strip based on the FBI, promised "FACTS—NOT FICTION!" At Hoover's urging, early strips showed panel after panel of FBI training. Once the stories began, he made sure the strip showed agents using science and acting as a team to chase down the crime-wave villains. Readers lost interest once the cartoon FBI nabbed the cartoon Dillinger, and the strip folded.

Hoover helped Hollywood make G-man movies as well. FBI agents unofficially served as advisers to guarantee that details were accurate. Hoover himself made a few quiet visits to Hollywood. But filmmakers knew movie fans wanted entertainment, not the accuracy Hoover demanded. Machine guns were more thrilling than a guy in a suit paging through a book of fingerprints. Hoover believed that even if the public didn't *want* his version of the FBI, it *needed* his version. At one point he wanted the FBI to make its own movies.

Not everyone approved of Hoover's actions. Some said he spent too much time promoting the FBI. Senator Kenneth Douglas McKellar of Tennessee asked Hoover if he had ever personally made an arrest. Hoover admitted he had supervised many cases but never made an arrest himself. The

admission embarrassed Hoover. He felt angry and insulted, perhaps with good reason. McKellar's question was not entirely fair. FBI agents were not even allowed to make arrests until 1934.

Hoover (right) worked with actor Edward G. Robinson on the set of the gangster movie Little Caesar.

Still, Hoover was now determined to make his first arrest. He set his sights on the latest Public Enemy Number One. The FBI wanted Alvin "Old Creepy" Karpis for a long list of crimes. Agents surrounded Karpis in New Orleans and took him without a fight. The *New York Times* headline read, "KARPIS CAPTURED IN NEW ORLEANS BY

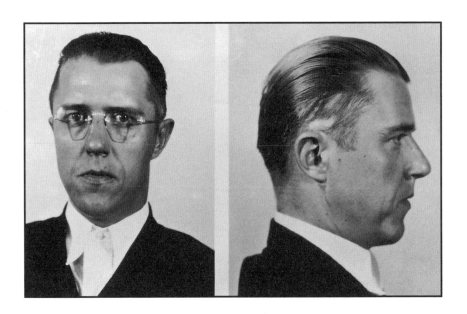

Alvin Karpis was the only man ever personally arrested by Hoover.

HOOVER HIMSELF." It was rumored Hoover and his public relations staff invented some details to juice up the story. "He was scared to death when we closed in on him," Hoover said in the newspaper article. "He shook all over—his voice, his hands, and his knees." Though Karpis disagreed with the story, Hoover's version became official FBI history.

In America in the 1930s, a person was considered famous when he made the cover of *Time* magazine. Hoover did so in 1935. With fame came many admirers. Universities lined up to give him honorary degrees. Groups invited him to lecture on crime. A 1936 poll of schoolboys named him the second-most admired man in America, after President Roosevelt.

The public wanted personal details about

Hoover to go along with the crime stories. One article read:

> *His name has probably made more headlines than any other except President Roosevelt, but those who know that he is a stamp and antique collector, that he is a baseball fan and an expert fisherman, could be assembled in a small drawing room.*

Hoover made famous friends. One of most important was Walter Winchell. In the 1930s, Americans got their news from newspapers and radio. Winchell was the most popular gossip columnist in both. On some weekends, Hoover and Winchell spent evenings at a New York City nightclub that catered to the rich and famous. Hoover wrote to Winchell:

> *I do get some real relaxation and enjoyment in attending some of the night clubs ... and I am looking forward to many evenings in the future when we can get together and have some real fun and settle the momentous questions of the nation.*

The two were personal friends, but they also shared a working relationship. Winchell gave the director favorable coverage in his column and on the radio. In return, Hoover passed on gossip that FBI agents dug up on politicians or celebrities.

But Hoover's most enduring friendship was with Clyde Tolson, an FBI agent who became Hoover's closest personal friend and business associate, replacing Frank Baughman who had gotten married.

Hoover and Tolson went everywhere together. Hoover's limousine picked Tolson up every morning and they lunched together every day. Five nights a week they shared dinner at a local restaurant.

Clyde Tolson (left) was Hoover's coworker and lifelong friend.

Careful to show respect in public, Tolson always walked a pace behind Hoover and addressed him as "Mr. Hoover." In more relaxed moments, though, he called him "Boss," "Eddie," or the family nickname, "Speed." Hoover liked to call Tolson "Junior." Hoover invented the job of assistant to the director especially for Tolson, making his friend the second most powerful man in the Bureau. And for more than 40 years, they worked together, lunched together, and vacationed together.

Hoover and Tolson enjoyed betting on horse racing and rarely missed a chance to visit the racetrack. According to official stories, Hoover never bet more than $2 on a race. Other stories, however, claimed that he used FBI agents to place secret bets for him that were much larger. Tolson often steered Hoover away from placing bets that were too risky.

In 1935, Hoover lost the person closest to him. Though he spent more time at work than at home, Hoover continued to live with his mother in the house in Seward Square. He called her every day when he was out of town and never returned home without a gift. In 1935, his mother became ill. She refused to see a doctor and slowly got sicker, most likely with cancer. Hoover was present when she died on February 22, 1938. ℘

7 A Threat to the Nation

Chapter

❧

In 1941, the United States entered World War II, which had been raging in Europe since 1939. While U.S. troops shipped out to fight in Europe and the Pacific, Hoover's attention was focused, as always, on enemies at home. The FBI continued to gather information on people and organizations that he believed posed a threat to the U.S. government. Hoover hired more agents to handle cases related to the war effort and requested that FBI agents be excused from military service.

The war ended in 1945 with America and its allies the winners. Almost immediately, the United States and its former ally, the communist Soviet Union, entered a new kind of conflict. The two nations became locked in a cold war, one fought

Wisconsin Senator Joseph McCarthy gave his name to an anti-communist era that destroyed many innocent lives.

with threats and economic pressure rather than with bullets and bombs. Both sides were powerful. Both had a vision of the world opposed by the other.

To Hoover and many others in the United States, Americans with "communist sympathies" were once again dangerous. Such people might become spies for the Soviets. To Hoover, being a good American meant being anti-communist.

No sooner had the Cold War begun than Hoover launched a campaign to educate the public on the communist threat. The campaign landed him on the cover of *Newsweek* magazine in 1947. In an essay, Hoover gave advice on how to fight the threat. He also included a second warning:

> *The known, card-carrying Communist is not our sole menace. The individual whose name does not appear on party [member lists] but who does the party's dirty work, who acts as an apologist for the party ... is a greater menace. These are the "communist sympathizers," "fellow travelers," and "communist stooges."*

At least 1 million Americans, he added, helped the communists in some way.

Certain politicians exaggerated the communist threat to increase their power. Others believed it was real, including Hoover. One former agent said:

You have to understand that Hoover was obsessed with what he called "com-monism," and he couldn't even pronounce the word properly. When someone is that fanatic, and you want to keep your job, you just go along with it.

A poster signed by Hoover encouraged Americans to help the FBI track down enemy agents.

WARNING
from the
FBI

The war against spies and saboteurs demands the aid of every American.

When you see evidence of sabotage, notify the Federal Bureau of Investigation at once.

When you suspect the presence of enemy agents, tell it to the FBI.

Beware of those who spread enemy propaganda! Don't repeat vicious rumors or vicious whispers.

Tell it to the FBI!

J. Edgar Hoover, *Director*
Federal Bureau of Investigation

The nearest Federal Bureau of Investigation office is listed on page one of your telephone directory.

Fear, suspicion, exaggeration, and politics all came together to create a second Red Scare that was even greater than the first.

One of the most controversial cases the Bureau investigated during this time involved a government official named Alger Hiss who was accused of spying for the Soviets. In 1948, Hiss went before Congress to deny the charges. His denial soon became famous:

> I am not and have never been a member of the Communist Party. I do not and have not adhered to the tenets of the Communist Party. I have never followed the Communist Party line.

Richard M. Nixon, a young congressman from California, led the charge against Hiss. Hoover provided Nixon and other anti-communist congressmen with information. Even when President Harry Truman forbade the FBI to share files with Congress, Hoover made sure helpful information from Hiss' files—though not the actual files—found its way to Nixon and others.

In his 1950 trial, Hiss was found guilty, not of spying but of lying under oath. Nixon flattered Hoover with the credit, saying:

> Mr. Hoover recognized the Communist threat long before other top officials

Alger Hiss spoke before Congress and denied any association with the Communist Party.

recognized its existence. ...The FBI in this trial did an amazingly effective job of ... developing the evidence which made the prosecution successful.

But the Hiss case was just the beginning. On February 9, 1950, Wisconsin Senator Joseph R. McCarthy spoke in Wheeling, West Virginia. What was supposed to be an ordinary speech was instead a statement that shook the country:

While I cannot take the time to name all the men in the State Department who have been named as members of the Communist Party and members of a spy ring, I have here in my hand a list of 205—a list of names that were known to the Secretary of State and who, nevertheless, are still working and shaping the policy of the State Department.

Senator McCarthy was a former judge and ex-Marine elected to the Senate in 1946. By the time of the Wheeling speech, he had accomplished little. He was up for reelection and needed an issue to run on. Communists in the government fit the bill.

Unfortunately for McCarthy, he had no facts to back up his charges. In fact, McCarthy knew little about communism. He asked Hoover for help. "This caused headlines all over the country," he told Hoover, "and I never expected it, and now I need some evidence to back up my statement." Hoover and McCarthy were friends. Both shared conservative political views and liked to bet on horse races. Hoover agreed to help.

No one played a more important role in McCarthy's anti-communist campaign than Hoover and the FBI. But Hoover preferred to keep his role hidden. "I would not want to be a party to any action which would 'smear' innocent individuals for the rest of their lives," he publicly said. Behind the scenes, though, he provided McCarthy with information and advice. One of Hoover's aides told McCarthy how to make his charges tougher to refute. It was hard to prove a person was a communist, the aide said. But the tiniest piece of information could be twisted to label that same person a "communist sympathizer." Whether it was true or false was not necessarily important. The *New York Times* recognized how the FBI operated and reported, "The FBI faithfully records everything everybody tells its agents about the person in question. It doesn't weigh or evaluate the data, separate the ... gossip from the ... fact."

Some people did resist McCarthyism. After his term ended, former President Truman blasted McCarthy in a televised speech that spoke for many Americans: "McCarthyism ... is the corruption of truth, the abandonment of our historical devotion to fair play. ... It is the spread of fear and the destruction of faith in every level of our society. ... This horrible cancer is eating at the vitals of America and it can destroy the great edifice of freedom."

The search for Reds spread across the country. Congressional committees, such as the House Un-American Activities Committee, held hearings to find communists in the United States. At the same time, Hoover and the FBI set up a new operation known as COINTELPRO (short for "counterintelligence programs") to disrupt the Communist Party from the inside. The Bureau hired people to join the

Hoover spoke to Congress about his belief in a communist threat to the United States.

party and then start arguments, spread rumors, and make accusations that would turn members against one another. They also leaked members' names to local papers. Even the rumor of a link to the Communist Party could cost a person his job, and the ongoing congressional investigations and COINTELPRO operations damaged or destroyed the careers of many innocent citizens.

Senator McCarthy's career, however, was flourishing, and he rode the Red Scare to reelection in 1952. While Hoover still preferred to work with him in secret, he did not shy away from McCarthy. He told a newspaper:

I view him as a friend and believe he so views me. Certainly he is a controversial man. He is earnest and he is honest. He has enemies. Whenever you attack Communists, Fascists, even the Ku Klux Klan, you are going to be the victim of ... extremely vicious criticism.

The McCarthy era lasted almost four years. The senator's charges made headlines, destroyed careers, divided the country, and eventually brought down McCarthy himself. In the end, he self-destructed. He angered President Dwight D. Eisenhower, a former Army general, when he accused the U.S. Army of hiding communists. But McCarthy committed another, far bigger mistake: He let it be known he had received information from FBI files. Hoover at once denied McCarthy had seen any files. That was the truth, though barely. McCarthy only saw information based on what was in the files.

Furious, Hoover cut off McCarthy's access to information. McCarthy became desperate. Televised hearings showed him insulting witnesses and making wild charges. The public and press, and finally the Senate, turned against him. Hoover, however, once again managed to escape the ugly situation with his position and his power intact. ✑

DIRECTOR
·
FEDERAL BUREAU
OF INVESTIGATION

8 THE RELUCTANT DIRECTOR

❦

By the 1950s, Hoover had become more powerful and more famous than ever. His new status as a national leader allowed him to relax. Coworkers thought he seemed to enjoy life more. At the same time, he fought harder than ever against criticism of the Bureau or himself. Agents often claimed that the worst sin in the FBI was to do or say something that could hurt the organization's image. Some critics believed fear of embarrassment made Hoover reluctant to assign the Bureau to certain kinds of cases—organized crime and civil rights, in particular.

Organized crime was known by many names: the Mob, the Syndicate, the Outfit, Cosa Nostra, and the Mafia. These groups controlled empires of gambling, theft, drug dealing, and other illegal activities that

Martin Luther King Jr. visited Hoover at the FBI office to discuss public comments Hoover made about him.

brought in hundreds of millions of dollars. Compared to the men behind the Mob, John Dillinger, Old Creepy Karpis, and Pretty Boy Floyd were second-rate crooks.

Not only did Hoover ignore these crime organizations, but he denied for years that they even existed. Few contradicted him. It was hard to argue with a man considered America's greatest crime fighter. In reality, organized crime was no mystery, not even to the FBI. Hoover himself was on hand when an infamous mobster named Louis Buchalter surrendered to authorities in 1939. Hoover's reluctance to pursue the Mob afterward confused and angered many people, including his own colleagues. An FBI assistant director explained:

> *He preferred his agents to spend their time on quick easy cases—he wanted results, predictable results.... [T]he Mafia is powerful. So powerful that entire police forces or even a mayor's office can be under Mafia control. That's why Hoover was afraid to let us tackle it. He was afraid that we'd [do] poorly.*

Others said he was too focused on communism. Hoover offered his own reasons. Crime was a local problem, he explained, and the law did not allow a federal agency such as the FBI to get involved.

In the late 1950s, several crime organizations

began to fight each other around New York City. Assassins shot down mob leaders in hotel lobbies and barbershops. On November 14, 1957, more than 100 Mob leaders met in Apalachin, New York. State police captured 62 of them at a roadblock. After this well-publicized event, the press and public

Mafia associate Vito Genovese was photographed after his 1955 arrest in New York City.

demanded to know what the FBI meant to do about organized crime.

At first the Bureau was caught by surprise. One investigator for Congress said:

> *I asked for files on each of [the mobsters] and [the FBI] didn't have any information, I think, on forty. ... The FBI didn't know anything, really, about these people who were the major gangsters of the United States.*

Hoover ordered FBI agents to put together a study of the Mob. Two weeks after the Apalachin meeting, offices throughout the country were told to gather information on mobsters. This soon included the use of secret microphones known as "bugs." Agents listening in were stunned to hear Mob leaders discussing past and future crimes, business dealings, and enemies and allies. Those allies, as the agents found out, included many public officials, from policemen and judges on up to governors and U.S. senators.

Using bugs to spy on Americans was illegal in all but a few situations. Because of that, the information the FBI heard through the microphones could not be used in court cases. It did, however, fill up FBI files. At times, bugs provided information that helped the Bureau prevent crimes. But for the most

FBI agents listened to messages being transmitted using the radio.

part, Hoover simply kept the files handy, in case the information were to become useful later.

Because the use of bugs remained secret, many complained that Hoover did nothing to fight organized crime. It was true that Hoover considered communists more dangerous than mobsters. Though

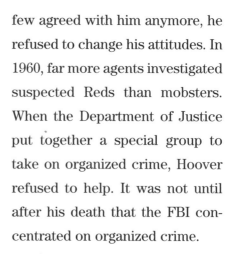

In the 1950s, a group of FBI employees researched and wrote a study of communism titled Masters of Deceit. Published in 1958, the book sold more than 2 million copies. Hoover was credited as the book's author, although he didn't write a single word. Agents joked that he never read the book, either.

few agreed with him anymore, he refused to change his attitudes. In 1960, far more agents investigated suspected Reds than mobsters. When the Department of Justice put together a special group to take on organized crime, Hoover refused to help. It was not until after his death that the FBI concentrated on organized crime.

Civil rights crimes were another type of case Hoover's Bureau tended to ignore. African-Americans had long suffered from unfair treatment and segregation. Prejudice existed everywhere, but worst of all in the South. Jim Crow laws made it legal to discriminate against African-Americans and keep them separate from whites. New attitudes and laws, however, were moving African-Americans closer to equal rights. Some whites in the South fought back against these changes. Since these people controlled many governments and police forces, African-Americans asked the federal government to step in and protect them. Civil rights leader Andrew Young said, "We thought of the FBI as our friends ... the only hope we had."

Hoover disagreed. He believed communists

were behind the civil rights movement. But, President John F. Kennedy supported increased civil rights. So did Hoover's new boss, Attorney General Robert Kennedy, the president's brother. Both ordered Hoover to get the FBI more involved.

Hoover (center back) and Attorney General Robert Kennedy (second from right) watch as President John F. Kennedy signs a bill into law.

79

King and other civil rights leaders organized the March on Washington to draw the government's attention to African-American unemployment and to urge Congress to pass a wide-ranging civil rights bill that President Kennedy had proposed. On August 28, 1963, more than 200,000 Americans, including many whites, gathered at the Lincoln Memorial. King's famous "I Have a Dream" speech, which defined the moral basis of the civil rights movement, was the high point of the event.

authorities who attacked civil rights marchers with fire hoses and the racists who murdered African-Americans. Instead he put King's friends under surveillance, including the use of bugs. Memo after memo on King's "communist ties" were sent to the Kennedys. Hoover even tried to stop the March on Washington, where King gave his famous "I Have a Dream" speech.

After the march, Hoover convinced Attorney General Kennedy to allow him to install microphones in King's hotel rooms. The bugs revealed information that could damage King's reputation. Hoover believed this information was the ammunition he needed to ruin King. In late 1964, someone at FBI headquarters sent King a package that contained information revealed by the bugging. It also included a letter that read in part:

> King, look into your heart. You know you are a complete fraud and a great liability to all of us Negroes. ... You are no clergy-

man and you know it. I repeat, you are a colossal fraud and an evil, vicious one at that. ... You are done. There is but one way out for you. You better take it before your filthy, abnormal, fraudulent self is bared to the nation.

King knew the FBI was behind the package and told friends he believed the FBI was trying to break him. But the attempts to start a scandal failed. When

Martin Luther King Jr. waved to supporters who marched on Washington on August 28, 1963.

the Bureau offered the evidence to reporters, all declined to take it.

Around the same time, Hoover publicly referred to King as the most notorious liar in the country. King responded gently:

> *I cannot conceive of Mr. Hoover making a statement like this without being under extreme pressure. ... I have nothing but sympathy for this man who has served his country so well.*

On November 22, 1963, President Kennedy was fatally shot while traveling in a motorcade through the streets of Dallas, Texas. Lee Harvey Oswald was arrested for the crime. Oswald was an admitted communist sympathizer who had once tried to become a citizen of the Soviet Union. This background, combined with other evidence, led many to believe that Oswald was part of a larger plot to kill the president.

The public was more critical of Hoover's comment. A newspaper cartoon showed him passing a wanted poster with his own picture and the caption, "His Own Worst Enemy #1." Still, Hoover continued to speak out against Dr. King.

After President Kennedy was assassinated in 1963, his vice president, Lyndon B. Johnson, became president. Johnson, a former senator from Texas, was an old supporter of Hoover's. He also had a thick file of his own at FBI headquarters. Determined to go down in history as the "civil rights president," Johnson ordered Hoover to pursue Southern racist groups. Hoover might have hesitated, as he had in the past, but Johnson had him at a disadvantage. On January 1, 1965, Hoover would turn 70 years old. By law, he had to retire. Johnson issued a special order to allow him to keep his position—but it could be cancelled at any time.

Hoover had no choice but to follow Johnson's orders. When three civil rights workers vanished in Mississippi, 500 FBI agents joined the case. Agents discovered the bodies buried in a dam and helped bring the killers to justice.

The Bureau used many of the same methods against the racist Klan that it had against Reds. This included informants and tapping phones. Klansmen who hid behind white sheets and hoods suddenly realized they could now be identified. The FBI made this clear when it sent unsigned postcards to known Klansmen at home and at work. The postcards told them that they were no longer safe behind their sheets. Receiving the postcard meant that someone—and someone in the FBI, at that—knew their identity.

This tactic yielded results. John Doar, the DOJ's civil rights director, said, "The Bureau did a real job. The violence subsided. ...The ... midnight group of killers ... [were] brought to courts for trial." ❧

9 THE MOST POWERFUL MAN IN AMERICA

Chapter

❦

When Richard Nixon became president in 1969, Hoover was 74 years old. The problems of old age had set in. In 1958, he had suffered a minor heart attack and high blood pressure continued to be a worry. Weight was an issue—he gave up favorite desserts like angel food cake and chocolate cream pie. Sometimes he could not catch his breath. He offset his lack of energy with mysterious vitamin injections. Hoover began to feel more pressure to retire, but he refused to consider it. He told others that although he had many plans for the future, none of them included retirement.

But the new president, Richard Nixon, had other ideas. Twenty years earlier, Hoover's information had helped Nixon become famous during the Alger

Friends and co-workers believed that retirement, not work, would kill J. Edgar Hoover.

President Nixon (left) hoped that Hoover would retire or resign.

Hiss investigation. But in recent years, Hoover and Nixon had disagreed about the use of bugging for political purposes. There were some things Hoover would not allow the FBI to do, even for the president, and so now Nixon plotted to replace him. At the same time, Congress and the press began to take a new interest in the ways the FBI did its work.

For years people had whispered about "the files." Very few people, however, knew what was in them. That made everyone, even presidents, reluctant to cross the man who kept the files— J. Edgar Hoover. For 50 years, agents had gathered all kinds of information—truth or gossip, serious or trivial. Some of it was gathered from newspaper articles or casual conversation. Some of it, though, was acquired in ways Hoover did not want revealed to the public: spying, opening mail, bugging, and tapping phones.

These secret files gave Hoover power. Some believed him to be the most powerful man in the United States. Only Hoover and a few high-ranking Bureau officials had access to these files. They used the information to pressure members of Congress, help allies, ruin enemies, and protect the director's job. With Congress' new interest in FBI procedures, the secrets the director had kept so long threatened to come into the open. Those secrets could ruin his reputation, and that of the FBI.

The thickest of the secret files were on political figures, like Franklin Roosevelt, or Hoover's enemies, like Martin Luther King Jr. But the FBI kept thousands of files on a long list of people both famous and ordinary. Scientist Albert Einstein had a file. So did baseball star Jackie Robinson, musician John Lennon, and actress Lucille Ball. Hoover even spied on his friends. Walter Winchell's file was 3,908 pages long. Criticizing the FBI or Hoover earned

The FBI kept a file on Brooklyn Dodgers star Jackie Robinson.

someone a file. So did holding political views that Hoover disagreed with.

Hoover knew he had to keep the files secret. Most Americans might agree with surveillance on groups like the Communist Party or the Ku Klux Klan. But keeping files on regular citizens sounded more like spying than law enforcement—especially since so much of what found its way into files was personal information that had nothing to do with crime. As one reporter put it:

> *FBI chief J. Edgar Hoover ... fiercely resisted a White House suggestion that he spare a few hundred agents to crack down on drug abuses. But he can spare agents to snoop into the [personal] habits, business affairs, and political pursuits of individuals who aren't even remotely involved in illegal activity.*

In the 1960s, Hoover ordered a series of new COINTELPRO operations—this time against racist organizations, people opposed to the Vietnam War, and other groups.

> *The FBI began collecting information on scientist Albert Einstein in 1933, when he arrived in the United States from Germany, and continued until his death in 1955. His FBI file was more than 1,800 pages long. According to the Bureau, Einstein participated in more than 30 groups sympathetic to communism. The FBI labeled Einstein a "risk," which prevented him from working on the atomic bomb project during World War II.*

As in the past, these counterintelligence programs were intended to disrupt the lives of their targets. M. Wesley Swearingen, a former FBI agent, explained:

> We would [say] that so-and-so is a member of the Communist Party, but we don't want you to fire him. We'd like you to keep an eye on him and if we get word that he might try to sabotage or something, we'll let you know right away. Most of the time I would do that. Of course, if you got someone with a miserable personality ... he didn't like Hoover, didn't like the FBI, didn't like the U.S. government—then you might pick on him and get him fired all the time.

On March 8, 1971, a group of burglars stole more than 1,000 documents from an FBI office in Pennsylvania. Week after week, copies of the documents were sent to public officials, reporters, and people the FBI had spied on. Newspapers printed the details of how the Bureau had illegally spied on Americans. One FBI official said that the burglary changed the FBI's image, possibly forever, in the minds of many Americans.

Denying the stories did not matter. Hoover was a lawyer. He knew all about evidence. And the newspapers had the evidence. Hoover rushed to cancel wiretaps, COINTELPROs—anything that might further damage the FBI's reputation. But there was more bad news to come. Two of his most trusted assistant directors, Cartha DeLoach and William Sullivan, left the Bureau. Sullivan soon began to tell some of the many secrets he knew.

Hoover knew that the FBI files revealed as much about the Bureau's activities as they did about the subjects, and so he took a drastic step. He began to destroy the files that had helped keep him in power so long. After two weeks, though, he gave up. He had only gotten as far as the letter *C*.

Hoover worked a full day on May 1, 1972. That night he ate dinner at Clyde Tolson's apartment. When he got home, he let out his two dogs, set the burglar alarm, and went to bed. He died of a heart attack during the night.

Despite their disagreements in recent years, President Nixon ordered a full state funeral for the

Though the FBI used a number of illegal methods to gather its information, there were some activities Hoover would not allow his agents to do. President Nixon organized his own group of investigators to carry out illegal operations against his enemies. This group was known as the "Plumbers," because its original mission was to stop press leaks. In 1972, the Plumbers broke into offices of the Democratic National Committee at the Watergate hotel in Washington, D.C. Though President Nixon was reelected that year, the scandal that resulted from the break-in would later force him to resign.

former FBI director. Only 21 Americans had ever lain in state in the Capitol Building. They had names like Lincoln, Eisenhower, and Kennedy. J. Edgar Hoover became the 22nd. Eight servicemen carried the coffin up the Capitol steps on a rainy Wednesday, May 3. Thousands of citizens, government officials, and former agents filed past to pay their respects. President Nixon spoke at the funeral on May 4. The service was broadcast live on all the television networks.

In the years that followed, the public began to learn more about the inner workings of the FBI. A new law required all government documents to be made available to anyone who requested them. Journalists and private citizens alike requested documents and files that revealed the FBI's surveillance and COINTELPRO operations, as well as bugging and other illegal activities. The resulting scandal forced the Bureau to make some changes. Still, when the government built a new headquarters for the FBI, it honored Hoover by naming the building after him. Despite the controversial new information, admirers pointed to how he had taken a corrupt agency and turned it into an organization respected around the world.

J. Edgar Hoover's 48-year career in government service transformed federal law enforcement. The controversial FBI director seemed to always walk

The J. Edgar Hoover Building in Washington, D.C., is the headquarters of the FBI.

the line between success and scandal, and in the end, he seemed to understand how history would remember him. As Hoover himself said, "I have a philosophy. You are honored by your friends and you are distinguished by your enemies. I have been very distinguished." ♋

HOOVER'S LIFE

1895

Born on January 1 in
Washington, D.C.

1913

Graduates from
Central High School
in Washington, D.C.

1900

1896

The Olympic Games
are held for the first
time in recent history
in Athens, Greece

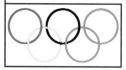

1913

Henry Ford begins to
use standard assem-
bly lines to produce
automobiles

WORLD EVENTS

1917

Graduates from George Washington University and takes a job as a clerk at the Department of Justice (DOJ)

1919–20

Takes a leading role in the Red Scare

1924

Appointed director of the Bureau of Investigation (BI)

1920

1917

Vladimir Lenin and Leon Trotsky lead Bolsheviks in a rebellion against the czars in Russia during the October Revolution

1923

French actress Sarah Bernhardt dies

HOOVER'S LIFE

1934

Becomes a celebrity as the DOI changes its name to the FBI and becomes the nation's authority on law enforcement and crimefighting technology

1933

Coins the term G-men in a press report

1930

1933

Nazi leader Adolf Hitler is named chancellor of Germany

1934

The British Road Traffic Act introduces driving tests for all motorists

WORLD EVENTS

1935

Is featured on the cover of *Time* magazine

1936

Makes his first and only arrest —of gangster Alvin "Old Creepy" Karpis

1948–49

Helps Congressman Richard Nixon investigate Alger Hiss

1940

1939

German troops invade Poland; Britain and France declare war on Germany; World War II (1939–1945) begins

1949

Birth of the People's Republic of China

HOOVER'S LIFE

1950–54

Provides Senator
Joseph McCarthy with
information on possi-
ble communists in the
U.S. government

1956

Launches the first of
the COINTELPRO
investigations

1950

1953

The first Europeans
climb Mount Everest

1959

Fidel Castro becomes
president of Cuba

WORLD EVENTS

1964

Feuds publicly and privately with Martin Luther King Jr.

1965

Reaches retirement age; remains as director of the FBI by special order of President Johnson

1972

Dies in his sleep in Washington, D.C., on May 2

1965

1966

The National Organization for Women (NOW) is established to work for equality between women and men

1971

First microprocessor is produced by Intel

NICKNAMES: Speed, J.E., The Boss

DATE OF BIRTH: January 1, 1895

BIRTHPLACE: Washington, D.C.

FATHER: Dickerson Naylor Hoover (1857–1921)

MOTHER: Annie Margaret Scheitlin Hoover (1860–1938)

EDUCATION: Master's degree in law, George Washington University, Washington, D.C.

DATE OF DEATH: May 2, 1972

PLACE OF BURIAL: Congressional Cemetery, Washington, D.C.

In the Library

Alonso, Karen. *The Alger Hiss Communist Spy Trial.* Berkeley Heights, N.J.: Enslow Publishers, 2001.

Denenberg, Barry. *The True Story of J. Edgar Hoover and the FBI.* New York: Scholastic, 1995.

Haskins, James. *The Life and Death of Martin Luther King, Jr.* New York: Harper Trophy, 1992.

January, Brendan. *The FBI.* New York: Franklin Watts, 2002.

Sherrow, Victoria. *Joseph McCarthy and the Cold War.* San Diego: Blackbirch Press, 1998.

Streissguth, Thomas. *J. Edgar Hoover: Powerful FBI Director.* Berkeley Heights, N.J.: Enslow Publishers, 2002.

Zeinert, Karen. *McCarthy and the Fear of Communism in American History.* Berkeley Heights, N.J.: Enslow Publishers, 1998.

Look for more Signature Lives
books about this era:

Andrew Carnegie: *Captain of Industry*

Carrie Chapman Catt: *A Voice for Women*

Henry B. Gonzalez: *Congressman of the People*

Langston Hughes: *The Voice of Harlem*

Douglas MacArthur: *America's General*

Eleanor Roosevelt: *First Lady of the World*

Elizabeth Cady Stanton: *Social Reformer*

ON THE WEB

For more information on *J. Edgar Hoover*, use FactHound to track down Web sites related to this book.

1. Go to *www.facthound.com*
2. Type in a search word related to this book or this book ID: 0756509971
3. Click on the *Fetch It* button.

FactHound will find the best Web sites for you.

HISTORIC SITES

Federal Bureau of Investigation
J. Edgar Hoover FBI Building
935 Pennsylvania Ave. NW
Washington, DC 20535
202/324-3447
To see the FBI building that was named after J. Edgar Hoover

Congressional Cemetery
1801 E St. SE
Washington, DC 20003
202/543-0539
To see the historic cemetery where J. Edgar Hoover and other famous Americans are buried

appeal
a request for a special court or official to review a previous legal decision

attorney general
the top law enforcement official in the United States

bug
a device that allows people to listen to sounds from a distant place

civil rights
rights promised under the Constitution, as well as other unofficial rights, such as the right to privacy

deport
to throw someone out of the country

motorcade
a procession of motor vehicles

public relations
the business of getting the public to feel good about a company, organization, or person

radical
someone who believes in making extreme changes to society and government

Red Scare
a period of intense worry about communists and communism; in American history, the Red Scare usually refers either to the years 1919–20, or the period between about 1947 and 1954

surveillance
a close watch kept over something or someone

sympathizers
people who share ideas, beliefs, or goals with others, but do not necessarily act on them

Chapter 1

Page 9, line 3: Bryan Burroughs. *Public Enemies: America's Greatest Crime Wave and the Birth of the FBI.* New York: Penguin, 2004, p. 209.

Page 10, line 8: Richard Gid Powers. *G-Men: Hoover's FBI in American Popular Culture.* Carbondale: Southern Illinois University Press, 1983, p. 123.

Page 12, line 3: *Public Enemies: America's Greatest Crime Wave and the Birth of the FBI*, p. 408 footnote.

Chapter 2

Page 17, line 13: Neal Jacob Kent. *America in 1900.* Armonk, N.Y.: M.E. Sharpe, 2000, p. 110.

Page 19, line 22: Jay Robert Nash. *Citizen Hoover: A Critical Study of the Life and Times of J. Edgar Hoover and His FBI.* Chicago: Nelson-Hall, 1972, p. 15.

Page 20, line 26: Richard Gid Powers. *Secrecy and Power: The Life of J. Edgar Hoover.* New York: Free Press, 1987, p. 23.

Page 22, line 22: Curt Gentry. *J. Edgar Hoover.* New York: W.W. Norton, 1991, p. 66.

Chapter 3

Page 30, line 5: *New York Times.* June 3, 1919.

Page 32, sidebar: *New York Times.* January 4, 1920.

Page 33, line 14: Robert K. Murray. *Red Scare: A Study in National Hysteria, 1919–1920.* New York: McGraw-Hill/University of Minnesota Press, 1964, p. 217.

Page 33, line 20: Max Lowenthal. *The Federal Bureau of Investigation.* New York: Sloane and Associates, 1950, p. 202.

Chapter 4

Page 39, line 9: Athan G. Theoharis and John Stuart Cox. *J. Edgar Hoover and the Great American Inquisition.* Philadelphia: Temple University Press, 1988, p. 63.

Page 40, line 20: *J. Edgar Hoover*, p. 127.

Page 42, line 3: Interview. *U.S. News and World Report.* Dec. 21, 1964, p. 40.

Page 42, line 16: *J. Edgar Hoover and the Great American Inquisition*, p. 85.

Chapter 5

Page 46, line 12: *Public Enemies: America's Greatest Crime Wave and the Birth of the FBI*, p. 58.

Page 46, line 15: Michael Wallis. *Pretty Boy: The Life and Times of Charles Arthur Floyd.* New York: St. Martin's Press, 1992, p. 322.

Page 47, line 9: *Public Enemies: America's Greatest Crime Wave and the Birth of the FBI*, pp. 12–13.

Page 49, line 9: Richard Hack. *Puppetmaster: The Secret Life of J. Edgar Hoover*, Beverly Hills, Calif.: New Millennium, 2004, pp. 148–149.

Chapter 6

Page 55, line 5: Ibid., p. 165.

Page 55, line 22: *G-Men: Hoover's FBI in American Popular Culture*, p. 142.

Page 58, line 3: *New York Times.* May 3, 1936, p. 1.

Page 59, line 3: Fred Cook. *The FBI Nobody Knows.* New York: Macmillan, 1964, p. 16.

Page 59, line 18: Neal Gabler. *Winchell: Gossip, Power, and the Culture of Celebrity.* New York: Knopf, 1994, p. 202.

Chapter 7

Page 64, line 15: J. Edgar Hoover. "How to Fight Communism." *Newsweek.* June 9, 1947, p. 30.

Page 65, line 1: Griffin Fariello. *Red Scare: Memories of the American Inquisition.* New York, W. W. Norton, 1995, p. 93.

Page 66, line 10: *Puppetmaster: The Secret Life of J. Edgar Hoover,* p. 254.

Page 66, line 26: *Secrecy and Power: The Life of J. Edgar Hoover,* p. 301.

Page 67, line 3: *J. Edgar Hoover,* p. 377.

Page 68, line 17: Thomas C. Reeves. *The Life and Times of Joe McCarthy.* New York: Stein and Day, 1982, p. 245.

Page 68, line 27: Fred J. Cook. *The Nightmare Decade.* New York: Random House, 1971, p. 255.

Page 69, sidebar: *The Life and Times of Joe McCarthy,* p. 529.

Page 69, line 15: *New York Times.* March 26, 1950.

Page 71, line 2: *Secrecy and Power: The Life of J. Edgar Hoover,* p. 321.

Chapter 8

Page 74, line 16: Sullivan, William C., with Bill Brown. *The Bureau: My Thirty Years Inside Hoover's FBI.* New York: W.W. Norton, 1979, p. 117.

Page 76, line 5: *J. Edgar Hoover,* p. 454 footnote.

Page 78, line 25: Ibid., p. 500.

Page 80, line 14: William W. Turner. "The Inside Story: An Agent's Dilemmas." In *Investigating the FBI.* Pat Watters and Stephen Gillers, eds. Garden City, N.Y.: Doubleday and Co., 1973, p. 96.

Page 80, line 25: Arlie Schardt. "Civil Rights: Too Much, Too Late." In *Investigating the FBI,* p. 187.

Page 82, line 25: Athan G. Theoharis, ed. *From the Secret Files of J. Edgar Hoover.* Chicago: Ivan R. Dee, p. 103.

Page 84, line 6: *Newsweek.* November 30, 1964, p. 30.

Page 85, line 25: "Civil Rights: Too Much, Too Late." In *Investigating the FBI,* pp. 197–198.

Chapter 9

Page 91, line 16: *J. Edgar Hoover,* p. 718.

Page 92, line 5: *Red Scare: Memories of the American Inquisition,* p. 90.

Page 95, line 3: *J. Edgar Hoover.,* p. 58.

Burroughs, Bryan. *Public Enemies: America's Greatest Crime Wave and the Birth of the FBI*. New York: Penguin, 2004.

Cook, Fred J. *The FBI Nobody Knows*. New York: Macmillan, 1964.

Cook, Fred J. *The Nightmare Decade*. New York: Random House, 1971.

Davis, James Kirkpatrick. *Spying on Americans: The FBI's Domestic Counterintelligence Programs*. New York: Praeger, 1992.

Fariello, Griffin. *Red Scare: Memories of the American Inquisition*. New York: W. W. Norton, 1995.

Garrow, David J. *The FBI and Martin Luther King*. New York: W.W. Norton, 1981.

Gentry, Curt. *J. Edgar Hoover: The Man and the Secrets*. New York: W.W. Norton, 1991.

Hack, Richard. *Puppetmaster: The Secret Life of J. Edgar Hoover*. Beverly Hills, Calif.: New Millennium, 2004.

Hoover, J. Edgar. "How to Fight Communism." *Newsweek*. June 9, 1947.

Lowenthal, Max. *The Federal Bureau of Investigation*. New York: Sloane and Associates, 1950.

Murray, Robert K. *Red Scare: A Study in National Hysteria, 1919–1920*. New York: McGraw-Hill/University of Minnesota Press, 1964.

Powers, Richard Gid. *G-Men: Hoover's FBI in American Popular Culture*. Carbondale: Southern Illinois University Press, 1983.

Powers, Richard Gid. *Secrecy and Power: The Life of J. Edgar Hoover*. New York: Free Press, 1987.

Sullivan, William C., with Bill Brown. *The Bureau: My Thirty Years Inside Hoover's FBI*. New York: W.W. Norton, 1979.

Summers, Anthony. *Official and Confidential: The Secret Life of J. Edgar Hoover*. New York: Putnam, 1993.

Theoharis, Athan G., ed. *From the Secret Files of J. Edgar Hoover*. Chicago: Ivan R. Dee, 1991.

Theoharis, Athan G., and John Stuart Cox. *J. Edgar Hoover and the Great American Inquisition*. Philadelphia: Temple University Press, 1988.

Watters, Pat, and Stephen Gillers (eds.). *Investigating the FBI*. Garden City, N.Y.: Doubleday and Co., 1973.